Redis Cookbook

Tiago Macedo and Fred Oliveira

Beijing · Cambridge · Farnham · Köln · Sebastopol · Tokyo

Redis Cookbook

by Tiago Macedo and Fred Oliveira

Printed in the United States of America.

Published by O'Reilly Media, Inc., 1005 Gravenstein Highway North, Sebastopol, CA 95472.

O'Reilly books may be purchased for educational, business, or sales promotional use. Online editions are also available for most titles (*http://my.safaribooksonline.com*). For more information, contact our corporate/institutional sales department: (800) 998-9938 or *corporate@oreilly.com*.

Editors: Andy Oram and Mike Hendrickson	**Cover Designer:** Karen Montgomery
Production Editor: Jasmine Perez	**Interior Designer:** David Futato
Proofreader: O'Reilly Production Services	

August 2011:   First Edition

Revision History for the First Edition:

2011-07-27 :   First release

2014-07-11 :   Second release

See *http://oreilly.com/catalog/errata.csp?isbn=9781449305048* for release details.

ISBN: 978-1-449-30504-8

[LSI]

Table of Contents

Preface

Introduction

Redis is a data structure server with an in-memory dataset for speed. It is called a data structure server and not simply a key value store because Redis implements data structures allowing keys to contain binary safe strings, hashes, sets and sorted sets, as well as lists. This combination of flexibility and speed makes Redis the ideal tool for many applications.

Redis first started in early 2009 as a key value store developed by Salvatore Sanfilippo in order to improve the performance of his own LLOOGG, an analytics product. Redis grew in popularity after getting support from people and companies in the developer world and has since been supported by VMware, who hired Salvatore and Pieter Noordhuis to work full-time on the project.

Today, Redis is used by companies large and small doing both large and small tasks. Companies like Engine Yard, Github, Craigslist, Disqus, Digg, and Blizzard are part of the growing list of Redis adopters. An extended list of people working with Redis is available on the project's official site at *http://redis.io*.

There are often several ways to solve problems using Redis. This book, while not a tutorial on Redis, key value stores, or data structures, gives you recipes for solving specific problems with Redis that you can then adapt to your own problem set. Many of these recipes have come up because we've used them in our own jobs, solving our own problems.

Each of these recipes solves a specific problem using Redis, including a quick introduction to the problem, the solution, and a longer discussion with insight into how the solution works. Redis is, while simple in nature, quite extensive when it comes to functionality to manipulate and store data. This volume will thus not cover every single command extensively. It will, however, give you the basics on solving specific problems with it, in hopes that our solutions guide you to your own.

Conventions Used in This Book

The following typographical conventions are used in this book:

Italic

Indicates new terms, URLs, email addresses, filenames, and file extensions.

`Constant width`

Used for program listings, as well as within paragraphs to refer to program elements such as variable or function names, databases, data types, environment variables, statements, and keywords.

`Constant width bold`

Shows commands or other text that should be typed literally by the user.

`Constant width italic`

Shows text that should be replaced with user-supplied values or by values determined by context.

 This icon signifies a tip, suggestion, or general note.

 This icon indicates a warning or caution.

Using Code Examples

This book is here to help you get your job done. In general, you may use the code in this book in your programs and documentation. You do not need to contact us for permission unless you're reproducing a significant portion of the code. For example, writing a program that uses several chunks of code from this book does not require permission. Selling or distributing a CD-ROM of examples from O'Reilly books does require permission. Answering a question by citing this book and quoting example code does not require permission. Incorporating a significant amount of example code from this book into your product's documentation does require permission.

We appreciate, but do not require, attribution. An attribution usually includes the title, author, publisher, and ISBN. For example: "*Redis Cookbook* by Tiago Macedo and Fred Oliveira (O'Reilly). Copyright 2011 Tiago Macedo and Fred Oliveira, 978-1-449-30504-8."

If you feel your use of code examples falls outside fair use or the permission given above, feel free to contact us at *permissions@oreilly.com*.

Safari® Books Online

 Safari Books Online is an on-demand digital library that lets you easily search over 7,500 technology and creative reference books and videos to find the answers you need quickly.

With a subscription, you can read any page and watch any video from our library online. Read books on your cell phone and mobile devices. Access new titles before they are available for print, and get exclusive access to manuscripts in development and post feedback for the authors. Copy and paste code samples, organize your favorites, download chapters, bookmark key sections, create notes, print out pages, and benefit from tons of other time-saving features.

O'Reilly Media has uploaded this book to the Safari Books Online service. To have full digital access to this book and others on similar topics from O'Reilly and other publishers, sign up for free at *http://my.safaribooksonline.com*.

How to Contact Us

Please address comments and questions concerning this book to the publisher:

> O'Reilly Media, Inc.
> 1005 Gravenstein Highway North
> Sebastopol, CA 95472
> 800-998-9938 (in the United States or Canada)
> 707-829-0515 (international or local)
> 707-829-0104 (fax)

We have a web page for this book, where we list errata, examples, and any additional information. You can access this page at:

> *http://www.oreilly.com/catalog/9781449305048*

To comment or ask technical questions about this book, send email to:

> *bookquestions@oreilly.com*

For more information about our books, courses, conferences, and news, see our website at *http://www.oreilly.com*.

Find us on Facebook: *http://facebook.com/oreilly*

Follow us on Twitter: *http://twitter.com/oreillymedia*

Watch us on YouTube: *http://www.youtube.com/oreillymedia*

Content Updates

July 11, 2014

- Recipes updated to comply with Redis 2.8
- Recipe 4.6 added for high availability with Sentinel
- Information added on Redis scripting, to reflect API changes and new libraries

Acknowledgements

We thank Pieter Noordhuis for thoroughly reviewing several chapters of our book, our editor Andy Oram for his work on making us look good, Salvatore Sanfilippo for his words of encouragement, and our respective companies for the extra free time to write this book.

CHAPTER 1

An Introduction to Redis

This chapter discusses some of Redis's basic concepts. We'll look into when Redis is a great fit, how to install the server and command-line client on your machines, and Redis's data types.

1.1. When to use Redis

Problem

Nearly every application has to store data, and often lots of fast-changing data. Until recently, most applications stored their data using relational database management systems (RDBMS for short) like Oracle, MySQL, or PostgreSQL. Recently, however, a new paradigm of data storage has emerged from the need to store schema-less data in a more effective way—NoSQL. Choosing whether to use SQL or NoSQL is often an important first step in the design of a successful application.

Solution

There are two important thing to consider when choosing whether to use SQL or NoSQL to store your data: its nature and your usage pattern. Some data is a great fit for a relational storage engine, while other data benefits from the schema-free nature of a NoSQL engine like Redis or its alternatives. If you don't rely on a particular RDBMS feature and need the performance or scalability of a NoSQL database, that might in fact be the ideal choice. So in order to decide whether your data should be stored in a RDBMS or NoSQL engine, you need to look into a few specific things that will help you make a decision. Also bear in mind that quite often the ideal solution will be to use both.

Are your application and data a good fit for NoSQL?

When working on the web, chances are your data and data model keep changing with added functionality and business updates. Evolving the schema to support these changes in a relational database is a painful process, especially if you can't really afford downtime —which people most often can't these days, because applications are expected to run 24/7. As a case in point, in a recent presentation on MongoDB, Jeremy Zawodny of Craigslist mentioned how changing the schema on their database typically takes a two month-long toll on their post archival service.

Examples of data that are a particularly good fit for nonrelation storage are transactional details, historical data, and server logs. These are normally highly dynamic, changing quite often, and their storage tends to grow quite quickly, further compounding the problem of adjusting the schema to store them. They also don't typically feel "relational" —that is, the data in them doesn't tend to fan out in relationships to other types of data. That's a good indication that they can use something other than a RDBMS.

Another way to gauge the fit for NoSQL is to look at whether you find yourself denormalizing your data for performance reasons, and no longer benefit from some of the advantages of a relational system, such as consistency and redundancy checks.

One thing to keep in mind is that NoSQL databases generally don't provide ACID (atomicity, consistency, isolation, durability), or do it only partially. This allows them to make a few tradeoffs that wouldn't be possible otherwise. Redis provides partial ACID compliance by design due to the fact that it is single threaded (which guarantees consistency and isolation), and full compliance if configured with `appendfsync always`, providing durability as well.

Performance can also be a key factor. NoSQL databases are generally faster, particularly for write operations, making them a good fit for applications that are write-heavy.

All this being said, and even though NoSQL feels more flexible, there are also great arguments to be made for storing relational data in a RDBMS. If you have predictable data that is a great fit for normalization, you can reap the benefits of using a relational data storage engine. Always look at the data before making a decision.

Don't believe the hype

NoSQL databases such as Redis are fast, scale easily, and are a great fit for many modern problems. But as with everything else, it is important to always choose the right tool for the job. Play to the strengths of your tools by looking at what you're storing, how often you'll access it, and how data (and its schema) might change over time.

Once you've weighted all the options, picking between SQL (for stable, predictable, relational data) and NoSQL (for temporary, highly dynamic data) should be an easy task. Doing this kind of thinking in advance will save you many headaches in future data migration efforts.

There are also big differences between NoSQL databases that you should account for. For example, MongoDB (a popular NoSQL database) is a feature-heavy document database that allows you to perform range queries, regular expression searches, indexing, and MapReduce (*http://en.wikipedia.org/wiki/MapReduce*). You should weigh all the factors when choosing your database. As we said earlier, the questions boil down to what your data looks like and what your usage pattern is.

For example, Redis is extremely fast, making it perfectly suited for applications that are write-heavy, data that changes often, and data that naturally fits one of Redis's data structures (for instance, analytics data). A scenario where you probably *shouldn't* use Redis is if you have a very large dataset of which only a small part is "hot" (accessed often) or a case where your dataset doesn't fit in memory.

1.2. Installing Redis

Problem

You want to install Redis on your computer.

Solution

There are several ways to install Redis on your computer or server, but the best and most flexible option is to compile it yourself. Nevertheless, depending on your distribution or operating system, there are other options.

Discussion

Compiling From Source

Redis evolves very quickly and package maintainers have a hard time keeping up with the latest developments. Since Redis doesn't have any external dependencies, compilation and installation are very straightforward, so we recommend you do it yourself. Redis should build cleanly in most Linux distributions, Mac OS X, Solaris, and Cygwin on Windows.

1. Downloading the source

   You can download Redis from the official site (*http://redis.io/download*) or directly from the Github project (*https://github.com/antirez/redis*), either using Git or your browser to fetch a snapshot of one the branches or tags. This allows you get to get development versions, release candidates, etc.

2. Compiling

   Redis compilation is straightforward. The only required tools should be a C compiler (normally GCC) and Make. If you want to run the test suite, you also need Tcl 8.5.

   After unpacking the source and changing your terminal path to the source directory, just type:

   ```
   make
   ```

   This will compile Redis, which on a modern computer should take less than 10 seconds. If you're using a x86_64 system but would like an x86 build (which uses less memory but also has a much lower memory limit), you can do so by passing along 32bit to Make:

   ```
   make 32bit
   ```

   After compiling Redis, particularly if you're building a development version, you should run the test suite to ensure that the server is behaving as expected.

   ```
   make test
   ```

3. Installing

   After compiling Redis, you can go ahead and run it:

   ```
   cd src && ./redis-server
   ```

   However, you might find it more convenient to install it to another location in your system. The Makefile wlll also help you do that:

   ```
   make install
   ```

   This will install Redis binaries to */usr/local/bin*. If you wish to install to another location, you can pass it to *make*. For instance:

   ```
   make install /opt/local
   ```

   This will install the binaries in */opt/local/bin*.

   After installating the Redis server, you should also copy the configuration file (*redis.conf*) to a path of your choice, the default being */etc/redis.conf*. If your configuration file is in a different path from the default, you can pass it along as a parameter to redis-server:

   ```
   /usr/local/bin/redis-server /alternate-location-for-redis-config.conf
   ```

Installing on Linux

Most modern Linux distributions have Redis packages available for installation, but keep in mind that these are normally not up-to-date. However, if you prefer to use these, the installation procedure is much simpler:

Debian/Ubuntu

```
sudo apt-get install redis-server
```

Fedora/Redhat/CentOS

```
sudo yum install redis
```

Gentoo

```
sudo emerge redis
```

This approach has a few advantages: by using your package management system, you can more easily keep software up-to-date, and you'll most likely get at least security and stability updates. Besides that, you'll also get startup scripts and an environment more suited to your distribution (user accounts, log files, database location, etc).

Installing on Windows

Although Redis is not officially supported on Windows for several reasons—notably the lack of a copy-on-write fork()—there is now a native port by Microsoft Open Technologies that implements CoW in userspace and therefore should have acceptable performance.

Beware that for performance and stability reasons, the Windows versions of Redis are not recommended for production use. Consider using a native or virtualized Linux/UNIX environment instead. Despite that, you might find these versions useful for development or testing.

The main disadvantage of using the Microsoft Open Technologies version is that, because it's a fork of Redis, there is a lag incorporating version updates from the original.

Being a native solution, compilation is simpler as it requires only Visual Studio. You can get the source and follow the project on Github (*https://github.com/MSOpenTech/redis*).

ServiceStack also maintains a page (*https://github.com/mythz/redis-windows*) with Vagrant (*http://www.vagrantup.com/*) boxes that automatically install and start Redis, making them a convenient solution for development purposes.

Installing on Mac OS X

There are several ways to install Redis on Mac OS X. They all require you to have the XCode developer tools installed, which includes libraries and compilers. If you are a developer on a Mac, chances are you already have this package installed. If you don't, you can either download it from Apple's developers website (*http://developer.apple.com*) or run "Install Developer Tools" on your Mac's installation DVDs.

You can manually compile Redis from source by following the steps earlier in this chapter. Most people, however, prefer the convenience of a package manager such as Fink, MacPorts, or Homebrew. A Redis package isn't available on Fink, so we'll cover the other two.

Installing through MacPorts. MacPorts defines itself as "an easy to use system for compiling, installing, and managing open source software." It is based on the FreeBSD Ports system, and to a large extent can be used in the exact same way.

In order to install Redis through MacPorts, you need to first install the package management system. There's an extensive guide on how to do that at guide.macports.org (*http://guide.macports.org/#using*). Once you've installed MacPorts, installing the Redis package is as simple as:

```
port install redis
```

Since Redis has no direct dependencies, the actual compilation and installation process is quite speedy. You will then be ready to start using Redis.

Installing through Homebrew. Homebrew is the latest entrant in the Mac package management scene. Being relatively new means that not every package you might be looking for is available on it—even though they make contributions very easy—but if you're looking for a tool that developers use often, chances are that it's going to be available through a Homebrew recipe.

You can install Homebrew by following the detailed instructions available over at Github, but it is usually as simple as running the following command:

```
ruby -e "$(curl -fsSLk https://gist.github.com/raw/323731/install_homebrew.rb)"
```

Once that's done, you'll be ready to install packages using the Homebrew recipes system. Installing Redis is just a matter of typing:

```
brew install redis
```

You can then run redis-server manually or install it into the Mac's own LaunchServices so that it starts when you reboot your computer. You can edit the configuration file */usr/local/etc/redis.conf* to tweak it to your liking, and then start the server:

```
redis-server /usr/local/etc/redis.conf
```

1.3. Using Redis Data Types

Problem

You need to understand Redis data types in order to make better use of them for specific applications.

Solution

Unlike most other NoSQL solutions and key-value storage engines, Redis includes several built-in data types, allowing developers to structure their data in meaningful

---

semantic ways. Predefined data types add the benefit of being able to perform data-type specific operations inside Redis, which is typically faster than processing the data externally. In this section, we will look at the data types Redis supports, and some of the thinking behind them.

Discussion

Before we dive into the specific data types, it is important to look at a few things you should keep in mind when designing the key structure that holds your data:

- Be consistent when defining your key space. Because a key can contain any characters, you can use separators to define a namespace with a semantic value for your business. An example might be using `cache:project:319:tasks`, where the colon acts as a namespace separator.

- When defining your keys, try to limit them to a reasonable size. Retrieving a key from storage requires comparison operations, so keeping keys as small as possible is a good idea. Additionally, smaller keys are more effective in terms of memory usage.

- Even though keys shouldn't be exceptionally large, there are no big performance improvements for extremely small keys. This means you should design your keys in such a way that combines readability (to help you) and regular key sizes (to help Redis).

With this in mind, keys like `c:p:319:t` or `user  123` would be bad—the first because it is semantically crude, and the latter because it includes whitespace. On the other hand, keys like `cache:project:319:tasks`, `lastchatmessage`, or `464A1E96B2D217EBE87449FA8B70E6C7D112560C` are good, because they're semantically meaningful. Note that the last example of an SHA1 hash is, while hard to guess and predict, semantically meaningful and quite useful if you are storing data related to an object for which you can consistently calculate a hash.

Strings

The simplest data type in Redis is a string. Strings are also the typical (and frequently the sole) data type in other key-value storage engines. You can store strings of any kind, including binary data. You might, for example, want to cache image data for avatars in a social network. The only thing you need to keep in mind is that a specific value inside Redis shouldn't go beyond 512MB of data.

Lists

Lists in Redis are ordered lists of binary safe strings, implemented on the idea of a linked list. This means that while getting an element by a specific index is a slow operation, adding to the head or tail of the data structure is extremely fast, as it should be in a database. You might want to use lists in order to implement structures such as queues, a recipe for which we'll look into later in the book.

Hashes

Much like traditional hashtables, hashes in Redis store several fields and their values inside a specific key. Hashes are a perfect option to map complex objects inside Redis, by using fields for object attributes (example fields for a car object might be "color", "brand", "license plate").

Sets and Sorted Sets

Sets in Redis are an unordered collection of binary-safe strings. Elements in a given set can have no duplicates. For instance, if you try to add an element wheel to a set twice, Redis will ignore the second operation. Sets allow you to perform typical set operations such as intersections and unions.

While these might look similar to lists, their implementation is quite different and they are suited to different needs due to the different operations they make available. Memory usage should be higher than when using lists.

Sorted sets are a particular case of the set implementation that are defined by a score in addition to the typical binary-safe string. This score allows you to retrieve an ordered list of elements by using the ZRANGE command. We'll look at some example applications for both sets and sorted sets later in this book.

CHAPTER 2

Clients

In this chapter, we'll look into some of the ways you can connect to Redis. We'll begin with the most basic option: Redis's command-line client, the `redis-cli` command. Then we'll look at ways to integrate Redis with common programming languages such as Ruby and Python.

2.1. Using Redis from the Command Line

Problem

Often you might find yourself in need of firing a simple Redis query, either to set or change a variable, flush a database, or perhaps take a look at your data. With Redis you can achieve this directly from the command line.

Solution

Redis ships with a command line client: *redis-cli*. Redis-cli is a fully featured interactive client, supporting line editing, history, and tab completion. By using `help` followed by a Redis command, you can also get help on how each command works.

You can use *redis-cli* to connect to a local or remote host Redis server and call commands by passing them as arguments (or piping them in) or by using its interactive mode.

Discussion

You can get a list of the command line options by typing:

```
redis-cli -h
```

The most typical usage scenarios would be something like the following, to connect to a remote server in interactive mode:

```
redis-cli -h serverip
```

The following connects to a local server running on a nondefault port in interactive mode:

```
redis-cli -p 6380
```

The following connects to a local server on the default port (6379), executes the *INFO* command, and returns you to your original shell:

```
redis-cli INFO
```

You can also use pipes and output redirection for a more powerful interaction:

```
cat command_list.txt | redis-cli > command_output.txt
```

2.2. Using Redis from Python with redis-py

Problem

You want to access and manipulate data in your Redis server with Python.

Solution

Install and use Andy McCurdy's redis-py (*https://github.com/andymccurdy/redis-py*) using *pip*, *easy_install*, or from the source code.

Discussion

Python's package index tool (*pip*) and *easy_install* make it trivial to install and start using redis-py. A couple of commands will get you going. Let's start by looking at how you install redis-py using *pip*:

```
pip install redis-py
```

Alternatively, if you're using *easy_install*, the installation command would be:

```
easy_install redis
```

From this point on, connecting to Redis in Python is as simple as issuing import redis, connecting to the server, and executing regular Redis commands. Here's an example:

```
>>> import redis
>>> redis = redis.Redis(host='localhost', port=6379, db=0)
>>> redis.smembers('circle:jdoe:soccer')
set(['users:toby', 'users:adam', 'users:apollo', 'users:mike'])
>>> redis.sadd('circle:jdoe:soccer', 'users:fred')
True
>>> redis.smembers('circle:jdoe:soccer')
set(['users:toby', 'users:adam', 'users:apollo', 'users:mike', 'users:fred'])
```

In order to squeeze a bit more performance out of your Redis and Python setup, you may want to install the Python bindings for Hiredis, a C-based Redis client library developed by the Redis authors. You can install the bindings by also using either *pip* or *easy_install*:

```
pip install hiredis
```

or using *easy_install*:

```
easy_install hiredis
```

redis-py will then automatically detect the Python bindings and use Hiredis to connect to the server and process responses—hopefully much faster than before.

2.3. Using Redis from Java with Jedis

Problem

You want to access and manipulate data in your Redis server using Java or another JVM-based language.

Solution

Download and use Jonathan Leibiusky's Jedis (*https://github.com/xetorthio/jedis*).

Discussion

If you are using Maven (*http://maven.apache.org/*), you can simply a new dependency to your project:

```
<dependency>
    <groupId>redis.clients</groupId>
    <artifactId>jedis</artifactId>
    <version>2.0.0</version>
    <type>jar</type>
    <scope>compile</scope>
</dependency>
```

If you're not using Maven, you can simply get a ready-to-use jar in the project's download page (*https://github.com/xetorthio/jedis/downloads*).

Once that is done, you should import it:

```
import redis.clients.jedis.*;
```

And then you're all set to go:

```
Jedis jedis = new Jedis("localhost");
jedis.set("foo", "bar");
String value = jedis.get("foo");
jedis.rpush("list", "element");
```

```
int length = jedis.llen("list").intValue();
String element = jedis.lpop("list");
```

Jedis supports all Redis commands, and adds sharding and connection pooling. Make sure you use a `JedisPool` connection pool if you are accessing the same connection from different threads as a single Jedis instances is not thread-safe.

2.4. Using Redis from Ruby with redis-rb

Problem

You want to access and manipulate data in your Redis server by using the Ruby programming language.

Solution

Use the official client, redis-rb (*https://github.com/redis/redis-rb*) to access and manipulate Redis data from Ruby applications.

Discussion

redis-rb is a full-fledged Redis client in Ruby created by Ezra Zygmuntowicz. In order to use it from Ruby, you should start by installing the Ruby gem with the `gem install redis` command. You can then use the Redis ruby gem to manipulate data in your Redis server instance. You can test your redis-rb installation straight from interactive Ruby (or `irb` for short):

```
> require 'rubygems'
=> true
> require 'redis'
=> true
```

If you get a true response when requiring the Redis gem, you are good to go. redis-rb makes it easy to call regular Redis methods by using the traditional Ruby language syntax. Here are a few examples where we use Redis's `set`, `get`, and `smembers` commands. Note that we start off by actually connecting to the redis-server instance by instantiating the Redis class:

```
> r = Redis.new
=> #<Redis client v2.2.0 connected to redis://127.0.0.1:6379/0 (Redis v2.2.11)>
> r.set 'hellofoo','hellobar'
=> "OK"
> r.get 'hellofoo'
=> "hellobar"
> r.sadd 'parkdogs', 'fido'
=> true
> r.sadd 'parkdogs', 'rudolph'
=> true
```

```
> r.sadd 'parkdogs', 'rex'
=> true
> r.smembers 'parkdogs'
=> ["rex", "rudolph", "fido"]
```

In these examples, we cut a little bit of the irb output for brevity and simplicity.

As you can see, using Redis from inside a Ruby script (or full-blown application) is quite trivial. In the next recipe, we'll look into how we can build upon what we just learned to use Redis from a Ruby on Rails-based application.

2.5. Using Redis with Ruby on Rails

Problem

You want to store and access data in Redis from a Ruby on Rails application.

Solution

Use the redis-rb library to access and manipulate Redis data from Ruby on Rails.

Discussion

If you already have a Ruby on Rails application, you can add Redis support to it by adding the following line to your Gemfile:

```
gem 'redis'
```

and by creating a file inside your config/initializers directory with the following initializer to connect your application to Redis:

```
$redis = Redis.new
```

This will create a global variable called `$redis` with which you can manipulate data and run commands on the engine. You can pass the `:host` and `:port` options to the `Redis.new` method in order to connect to a specific host and port instead of the default `localhost:6379`. redis-rb also lets you connect to Redis by using a Unix socket by passing the parameter :path.

Once these two steps are done, you are ready to start using Redis from Ruby on Rails. You can test out your setup by accessing and using the `$redis` variable from your Rails console by running:

```
rails console
```

and exploring Redis commands to get and set specific keys, hashes, sets, or lists.

Adding Redis functionality to ActiveRecord models

Let's imagine you have a User model and a Book model and you wanted to store a list of books that person owns by using a Redis set, thus allowing you to do creative things like seeing books users have in common easily. In this case, you could implement the following methods in the User model:

```
class User < ActiveRecord::Base
  def books
    b = $redis.smembers("books:#{self.id}")
    Book.where :id => b
  end
  def addbook(book)
    $redis.sadd("books:#{self.id}", book.id)
  end
  def delbook(book)
    $redis.srem("books:#{self.id}", book.id)
  end
  def common(user)
    c = $redis.sinter("books:#{self.id}", "books:#{user.id}")
    Book.where :id => c
  end
end
```

From this point, on it would be trivial to use the methods we just implemented from anywhere in our application, or from the Rails console. You could specify things like User.first.books to grab the first user's list of books, or maybe User.first.addbook(Book.first) to add the first book on your database to your user's collection.

CHAPTER 3

Leveraging Redis

In this chapter, we'll look into how we can leverage Redis's data structures, speed, and flexibility to create complex systems and functionality, typically in a fraction of the time we'd spend doing the same with a RDBMS. We'll start by looking at ways to store simple data sets, and work up from there in terms of complexity and interest.

3.1. Using Redis as a Key/Value Store

Problem

Most applications need to store temporary data about usage, configuration, or other relevant information that might not be a great fit for the fixed structure of relational databases. Traditionally, developers have resorted to hacking a table structure to accommodate this data and using MySQL or another RDBMS to store it. In this recipe, we'll look at how we can use Redis and its built-in data types to store application data in a lighter, faster, and looser manner.

Solution

Redis positions itself not simply as a key/value store but as a server for data structures as well. This means that on top of typical key/value store functionality, it gives you several ways to store and manipulate application data. We'll use these structures and commands to store application sample data: as examples, we'll store usage counters in regular keys, user objects in Redis hashes, and a circle-of-friend implementation (like Google+) using sets.

Discussion

Storing application usage counters

Let's begin by storing something quite basic: counters. Imagine we run a business social network and want to track profile/page visit data. We could just add a column to whatever table is storing our page data in our RDBMS, but hopefully our traffic is high enough that updates to this column have trouble keeping up. We need something much faster to update and to query. So we'll use Redis for this instead.

Thanks to the atomicity of Redis commands (see Recipe 1.3 for more about data types and atomicity), we know that if we store a counter key, we can use commands such as INCR (or INCRBY) and DECR (or DECRBY) to increment or decrement its contained value. So by designing a proper namespace for our data, maintaining our counters becomes a trivial one-operation endeavor.

There's no actual convention for organizing keys in systems like Redis, but a lot of people (including the authors) like to build keys out of keywords separated by colons, so we'll do that here. To store our social network page visit data, we could have a key namespace such as `visits:pageid:totals`, which for a page ID of 635 would look like `visits:635:totals`. If we already were storing visit data somewhere, we can first seed redis with that data by setting our keys to the current values:

```
SET visits:1:totals 21389
SET visits:2:totals 1367894
(...)
```

On a visit to a given page, a simple INCR command would update the counter in Redis:

```
INCR visits:635:totals
```

We could then grab the page visits for any page, at any time by doing a simple GET command by key:

```
GET visits:635:totals
```

You can also be smarter about the number of commands you run. Let's say you're showing the visitor himself how many visits the page he's looking at has had. Naturally, you'll be counting his own visit too, so you wouldn't even have to do the last GET: you can take advantage of the return value from the INCR command because it returns the post-increment count. A simple pseudocode for visits and counters could look like this:

1. The visitor requests the page.

2. We INCR the visits counter related to the page (INCR `visits:635:totals`, for instance).

3. We capture the return value of the INCR command.

4. We show the user the page with the return value.

This way we guarantee that the user always sees real live counter data when looking at the page, and that his own visited is counted too—all with a single Redis command.

Storing object data in hashes

As discussed in Recipe 1.3, Redis's implementation of hashes makes for a perfect solution to store the object data applications typically use. In the following example, we'll look into how we might use hashes to store information on users in a given system.

We'll begin by designing a key namespace to store our users. As before, we'll be separating keywords with colons to generate a rich key that makes sense in our system. For the sake of this recipe, we'll go with something simple like keys in the form of users:*alias*, where *alias* is a binary-safe string. So to store information about a user called John Doe, we might build a hash called users:jdoe.

Let's also assume we want to store a number of fields about our users, such as a full name, email address, phone number, and number of visits to our application. We'll use Redis's hash management commands—like HSET, HGET, and HINCRBY—to store this information.

```
redis> hset users:jdoe name "John Doe"
(integer) 1
redis> hset users:jdoe email "jdoe@test.com"
(integer) 1
redis> hset users:jdoe phone "+1555313940"
(integer) 1
redis> hincrby users:jdoe visits 1
(integer) 1
```

With our hash built and in place, we can fetch single fields with HGET or the full hash by using the HGETALL command, as exemplified here:

```
redis> hget users:jdoe email
"jdoe@test.com"
redis> hgetall users:jdoe
1) "name"
2) "John Doe"
3) "email"
4) "jdoe@test.com"
5) "phone"
6) "+1555313940"
7) "visits"
8) "1"
```

There are auxiliary commands like HKEYS, which return the keys stored in a particular hash, and HVALS, which returns only the values. Depending on how you want to retrieve your data, you may find it useful to use HGETALL or one of these to retrieve data from Redis into your application.

```
redis> hkeys users:jdoe
1) "name"
2) "email"
3) "phone"
4) "visits"
redis> hvals users:jdoe
1) "John Doe"
2) "jdoe@test.com"
3) "+1555313940"
4) "1"
```

For a list of additional commands to manage our users hash, peruse the Redis official documentation for hash commands (*http://redis.io/commands#hash*), which includes its own set of examples on managing data with hashes.

Storing user "Circles" using sets

To complete our look at some typical ways to store data in Redis, let's look at how we can use Redis's support for sets to create functionality similar to the circles in the recently launched Google+. Sets are a natural fit for circles, because sets represent collections of data, and have native functionality to do interesting things like intersections and unions.

Let's begin by defining a namespace for our circles. We want to store several circles for each of our users, so it makes sense for our key to include a bit about the user and a bit about the actual circle. As an example, John Doe's family circle might have a key like circle:jdoe:family. Similarly, his soccer practice buddies might be listed in a set with the key circle:jdoe:soccer. There's no set rule for key design, so always design them in a way that is meaningful to your application.

Now that we know which keys to store our sets in, let's create John Doe's family and soccer practice sets. Inside the set itself, we can list anything from user IDs to references to other keys in Redis, so we'll do the latter because it makes sense for us. This way if we want to grab a list of users that belong to John's family circle and show information about them, we can use the result of our set operation to then grab the actual hashes for each user (which might be stored as described in the previous section).

```
redis> sadd circle:jdoe:family users:anna
(integer) 1
redis> sadd circle:jdoe:family users:richard
(integer) 1
redis> sadd circle:jdoe:family users:mike
(integer) 1
redis> sadd circle:jdoe:soccer users:mike
(integer) 1
redis> sadd circle:jdoe:soccer users:adam
(integer) 1
redis> sadd circle:jdoe:soccer users:toby
(integer) 1
redis> sadd circle:jdoe:soccer users:apollo
(integer) 1
```

Keep in mind that in the examples above we should be normalizing the members of our set by using actual numbers for IDs rather than users:name. While the example above works great, it may be a good idea for performance reasons to sacrifice a bit of readability for more speed and memory efficiency.

Now we have a set called circle:jdoe:family with three values (in our case, these are users:anna, users:richard, and users:mike) and a second one called circle:jdoe:soccer with four values (users:mike, users:adam, users:toby, and users:apollo). The values themselves are only strings, but by using strings that are meaninful to us (they're similar to our key design for user hashes), we can use the result of the SMEMBERS command to then get information on specific users. Here's an example:

```
redis> smembers circle:jdoe:family
1) "users:richard"
2) "users:mike"
3) "users:anna"
redis> hgetall users:mike
(...)
```

Now that we know how to store information in sets, we can expand on this knowledge and do interesting things like getting people who belong in both of John Doe's sets (by intersecting our family and soccer sets), or getting a full list of everyone John Doe has added to circles in our system (by doing a union of John's sets):

```
redis> sinter circle:jdoe:family circle:jdoe:soccer
1) "users:mike"
redis> sunion circle:jdoe:family circle:jdoe:soccer
1) "users:anna"
2) "users:mike"
3) "users:apollo"
4) "users:adam"
5) "users:richard"
6) "users:toby"
```

According to our results, Mike is in both John Doe's family and soccer circles. By doing a union of the two circles, we also get a full list of John's friends in our system.

As you can see, Redis's sets make it extremely easy to do what would normally involve a number of queries in a typical RDBMS. It also does it extremely fast, making it an ideal candidate to implement applications that require managing (and doing operations with) sets. Circles are one example, but things like recommendations or even text search are also good fits for sets. We'll look at both of these examples in depth in later recipes.

Quick Reference for Key Operations

SET *key value* (http://redis.io/commands/set)
> Sets the key to hold the given value. Existing data is overwritten (even if of a different data type).

GET *key (http://redis.io/commands/get)*
    Returns the content held by the key. Works only with string values.

INCR *key (http://redis.io/commands/incr)*
    Increments the integer stored at *key* by 1.

INCRBY *key value (http://redis.io/commands/incrby)*
    Performs the same operation as INCR, but incrementing by *value* instead.

DECR *key (http://redis.io/commands/decr)*
    Decrements the integer stored at *key* by 1.

DECRBY *key value (http://redis.io/commands/decrby)*
    Performs the same operation as DECR, but decrementing by *value* instead.

3.2. Inspecting Your Data

Problem

While developing (or perhaps debugging) with Redis, you may find you need to take a look at your data. Even though it's not as simple (or powerful) as MySQL's SHOW TABLES; and SELECT * FROM table WHERE conditions; commands, there are ways of viewing data with Redis.

Solution

The Redis command that allows you to list your data is the KEYS command. Use it with the supported wildcard matchers. Thus, the following command:

```
KEYS *
```

will return all the keys in your database. However, that is not enough, as you still may not know what the key type is. That's what the TYPE command is for:

```
TYPE keyname
```

This will tell you whether that key is a string, hash, list, set, or zset.

In case you need to know the last time that some object stored at a key was either read or written to, you can leverage the OBJECTccommand:

```
OBJECT IDLETIME keyname
```

Discussion

The wildcard syntax of the KEYS command is limited but quite useful. It supports queries like:

```
KEYS h*llo
```
Returns all keys starting in h and ending in llo.

```
KEYS h?llo
```
Returns keys that start with h, end with llo, and have exactly one character between them.

```
KEYS h[ae]llo
```
Returns only the keys hallo and hello, if they exist.

Keep in mind that every time you use the KEYS command, Redis has to scan all the keys in the database. Therefore, this can really slow down your server, so you probably shouldn't use it as a normal operation. If you need a list of all your keys (or a subset) you might want to add those keys to a set and then query it.

Something else that might be useful if you're debugging a running application is the MONITOR command: it outputs the commands being sent to the server in real time.

Quick Reference for Debugging

KEYS *pattern* (*http://redis.io/commands/keys*)
 Lists all the keys in the current database that match the given pattern.

TYPE *key-name* (*http://redis.io/commands/type*)
 Returns the type of the key. Possible types are: string, list, hash, set, zset, and none.

OBJECT (*http://redis.io/commands/object*)
 Allows you to inspect internal details of the object associated with that key. Supports 3 subcommands: REFCOUNT, ENCODING, and IDLETIME.

MONITOR (*http://redis.io/commands/monitor*)
 Outputs the commands received by the Redis server in real time.

3.3. Implementing OAuth on Top of Redis

Problem

In this recipe, we'll implement a data model and interaction to support an OAuth v1.0a API. This is usually achieved on top of MySQL or another RDBMS, but we'll leverage Redis's data structures for a more efficient implementation.

Solution

We won't be implementing the API or the OAuth interaction itself. Here we're interested only in the data required for this sort of scenario. We'll be storing five types of data in Redis:

    consumer keys
    consumer secrets
    request tokens
    access tokens
    nonces

So the needs are as follows: applications (consumers) are identified by their key and secret, of which they have exactly one pair. Those consumers can have as many request and access tokens as they desire, and the nonces should be unique per consumer/time-stamp pair.

These types of data will be stored in hashes, sets, and strings depending on their specific requirements and interactions.

Discussion

Initial setup

To start with, consumers must enter their data before they issue a request. Let's put this data in a hash with the consumer information. The *key* is the one we've stored for the particular consumer when he or she registered with our system:

```
HMSET /consumers/key:dpf43f3p2l4k3l03
    secret kd94hf93k423kf44 created_at 201103060000
    redirect_url http://www.example.com/oauth_redirect name test_application
```

 Please ignore newlines in commands; they're only for styling purposes. A command should be issued all on one line.

This command gives us, for every application, a hash containing its "general" data, which can be extended over time. The same could be achieved in Memcache either by storing all the values in different keys or by storing the data in some format like JSON or YAML.

Quick Reference for Adding Values to Sets

HSET *hash-name key value* (http://redis.io/commands/hset)
> Sets a value on a hash with the given key. As with other Redis commands, if the hash doesn't exist, it's created.

HMSET *hash-name key1 value1 [key2 value2 ...]* (http://redis.io/commands/hmset)
> Allows you to set several values in a hash with a single command.

Getting a request token

In order to get a request token, consumers send their key, a timestamp, a unique generated nonce, a callback url, and a request signature that is a hash of the request path and parameters using the consumer secret. (For security purposes, the consumer secret is never sent—it's a pre-shared secret since both parts know it).

The API provider needs to verify that the signature is correct using the key and secret, check whether this nonce/timestamp combination was used previously (to prevent replaying), and generate a new request token.

In order to do so, the server needs to fetch the consumer data:

```
HGETALL /consumers/key:dpf43f3p2l4k3l03
```

and then check that this nonce hasn't been used yet:

```
SADD /nonces/key:dpf43f3p2l4k3l03/timestamp:20110306182600 dji430splmx33448
```

Using a set to store the nonce data has a few advantages. First, sets assure uniqueness (we'll see in a minute how to tell whether the element was present already). Also, we can delete all the nonces for past requests after a chosen period of time, by setting expiration times on each one. For this application, let's make the expiration time 30 minutes.

```
EXPIRE /nonces/key:dpf43f3p2l4k3l03/timestamp:20110306182600 1800
```

Now, if someone was to attempt to replay this request by sending the same timestamp and nonce, issuing the same SADD command as before would return 0, indicating that this value was already present in the set. Should this happen, the provider should refuse to generate a new token.

After validating all the data, we need to create a token and matching secret:

```
HSET /request_tokens/key:dpf43f3p2l4k3l03 hh5s93j4hdidpola hdhd0244k9j7ao03
```

Quick Reference for Authorization Algorithm

HGETALL *hash-name* (*http://redis.io/commands/hgetall*)
: Returns all the key/value pairs in the given hash.

SADD *set-name element* (*http://redis.io/commands/sadd*)
: Adds the element to the given set unless it's already a member. The return value is 1 if the element is added and 0 if it was already a member.

EXPIRE *key seconds* (*http://redis.io/commands/expire*)
: Sets an expiration timeout on a key, after which it will be deleted. This can be used on any type of key (strings, hashes, lists, sets or sorted sets) and is one of the most powerful Redis features.

EXPIREAT *key timestamp* (*http://redis.io/commands/expireat*)
: Performs the same operation as EXPIRE, except you can specify a UNIX timestamp (seconds since midnight, January 1, 1970) instead of the number of elapsed seconds.

TTL *key* (*http://redis.io/commands/ttl*)
: Tells you the remaining time to live of a key with an expiration timeout.

PERSIST *key* (*http://redis.io/commands/persist*)
: Removes the expiration timeout on the given key.

Redirections and consent

After successfully retrieving the request token, the consumer should redirect the user to the API provider, which will authenticate the user and authorize the application to access the user's data. Should the user grant his permission, we'll have to store it:

```
SET /authorizations/request_token:hh5s93j4hdidpola 16
```

Once that is done, we can redirect the user to the redirect URL we stored:

```
HGET /consumers/key:dpf43f3p2l4k3l03 redirect_url
```

Exchanging the request token for an access token

The access tokens are what the consumers need to authenticate with the API. These are obtained by submitting the consumer key, request token, and secret that were previously fetched and generating an access token. Most APIs that rely on OAuth do so for authentication purposes, so we'll also check whether this access token was authorized by a user.

```
HGETALL /consumers/key:dpf43f3p2l4k3l03
```

As for the previous operations, we need to check whether the consumer key is valid and matches an existing application.

```
HGET /request_tokens/key:dpf43f3p2l4k3l03 hh5s93j4hdidpola
```

We also need to check the request token and a failure to find it would probably mean someone is attempting to reuse a request token which is not allowed by the spec.

```
GET /authorizations/request_token:hh5s93j4hdidpola
```

The last thing we need to check is which user authorized this application.

```
SADD /nonces/key:dpf43f3p2l4k3l03/timestamp:20110306182700 kllo9940pd9333jh
EXPIRE /nonces/key:dpf43f3p2l4k3l03/timestamp:20110306182600 1800
```

Once again, the nonce should be unique for this consumer—the output of SADD suffices as sets assure uniqueness. A failure in any of the checks implies an invalid request and therefore we shouldn't generate an access token. If everything is OK, we can proceed:

```
HMSET /access_tokens/consumer_key:dpf43f3p2l4k3l03/access_token:nnch734d00sl2jdk
    secret pfkkdhi9sl3r4s00 user_id 16 created_at 20110306182600
HDEL /request_tokens/key:dpf43f3p2l4k3l03 hh5s93j4hdidpola
DEL /authorizations/request_token:hh5s93j4hdidpola
```

Perhaps somewhere in our application we allow users to see which applications have access to their credentials. To facilitate the retrieval of that information, let's add it to a hash of client applications:

```
HSET /users/user_id:16/applications dpf43f3p2l4k3l03 nnch734d00sl2jdk
```

A follow-up feature would be to allow users to revoke access to these applications. Doing so is trivial:

```
HDEL /users/user_id:16/applications dpf43f3p2l4k3l03
DEL /access_tokens/consumer_key:dpf43f3p2l4k3l03/access_token:nnch734d00sl2jdk
```

Our application logic might also define different expiration times for each new token, perhaps even at the user's request. Let's say that in this case the user gave permission for 24 hours (86,400 seconds):

```
EXPIRE /access_tokens/consumer_key:dpf43f3p2l4k3l03/access_token:nnch734d00sl2jdk
    86400
```

Beware of one detail: if you are expiring the access tokens, you need either to check for their existence (and remove them from the hash if they're absent) before presenting the user with the list of authorized applications, or to do a regular clean-up operation that checks that the keys in the `/users/user_id:16/applications` hash are still valid.

Quick Reference for Hash Operations

HGET *hash-name key (http://redis.io/commands/hget)*
    Returns the value at *key* in the given hash.

> HDEL *hash-name key* (*http://redis.io/commands/hdel*)
>   Deletes a key/value pair in the given hash.

API Access

When the consumer is accessing the API, the process should be really simple: validate the keys, secrets, signatures, and nonce.

```
HGETALL /consumers/key:dpf43f3p2l4k3l03
HGETALL /access_tokens/key:dpf43f3p2l4k3l03/access_token:nnch734d00sl2jdk
SADD /nonces/key:dpf43f3p2l4k3l03/timestamp:20110306182800 kllo9940pd9333jh
EXPIRE /nonces/key:dpf43f3p2l4k3l03/timestamp:20110306182600 1800
```

3.4. Using Redis's Pub/Sub Functionality to Create a Chat System

Problem

You want to leverage Redis's pub/sub functionality to create a light real-time chat system with Node.js and Socket.IO.

Solution

Since Redis has native support for the publish/subscribe (or pub/sub) pattern, we can easily use it in conjunction with Node.js and Socket.IO to quickly create a real-time chat system.

The publish/subscribe pattern defines a way in which receivers subscribe to messages that match a specific pattern (for instance, messages that are sent to a specific "channel"), and a way for an emitter to send messages to a message cloud. When a message hits that cloud, clients that subscribe to messages of that kind will get the message. The pattern allows then for emitters and clients to be loosely coupled—they don't need to know each other. They just need to be able to send messages in a given pattern, and receive messages that match that pattern.

For a better understanding of how Publish/Subscribe works, see the Wikipedia page (*http://en.wikipedia.org/wiki/Publish/subscribe*).

Redis has direct support for the pub/sub pattern, meaning that it lets clients subscribe to specific channels matching a given pattern, and to publish messages to a given channel. This means that we can easily create channels like "chat:cars" for car-talk, or "chat:sausage" for food-related conversation. The channel names are not related to the Redis keyspace so you don't have to worry about conflicts with existing keys. The pub/sub functionality is supported by the following Redis commands:

PUBLISH
> Publishes to a specific channel

SUBSCRIBE
> Subscribes to a specific channel

UNSUBSCRIBE
> Unsubscribes from a specific channel

PSUBSCRIBE
> Subscribes to channels that match a given pattern

PUNSUBSCRIBE
> Unsubscribes from channels that match a given pattern

With this knowledge, it is trivial to implement chat and notification systems, either for end-users or to stream messages between logical parts of applications. Pub/sub can even be used as a building block of a robust queueing system. Let's look at our simple implementation of an instant messaging chat system.

On the server side, Node and Socket.IO will take care of the network layer, and Redis will act as a straightforward implementation of pub/sub that delivers messages between clients. On the client side, we'll use a hint of jQuery to process messages, and send data to the server.

Discussion

For this recipe, we'll assume that you have a recent installation of Node.js, as well as *npm* in order to install the necessary node libraries to support the chat system (Socket.IO and Redis). We'll start by looking at how we install the necessary software to build the chat solution, and then go through the code for the server and client sides of the software.

Installing the necessary software

Let's start off by installing the necessary node libraries using *npm*:

```
npm install socket.io
npm install redis
```

Implementing the server side code

On the server side, we'll be running Redis and creating a Javascript file that we'll run with Node.js. This piece of code will take care of setting up a connection to Redis and listening on a given port for connecting clients (either using websockets or flash—this choice will be handled transparently by Socket.IO). Let's go through our necessary JavaScript code. Create a *chat.js* file containing the following code:

```
var http = require('http'),
io = require('socket.io'),
```

```
    redis = require('redis'),
    rc = redis.createClient();
```

These lines require the libraries we installed and create the variables we'll use to access Redis and Socket.IO. We'll access Redis with the "redis" variable, and "io" will let us access all the sockets that are connected to our server (web clients, who visit our chat page).

The next thing we must do in our code is to set up an HTTP server system on top of which Socket.io will do its websocket magic. Here are the lines to do that:

```
server = http.createServer(function(req, res){
    // we may want to redirect a client that hits this page
    // to the chat URL instead
    res.writeHead(200, {'Content-Type': 'text/html'});
    res.end('<h1>Hello world</h1>');
});

// Set up our server to listen on 8000 and serve socket.io
server.listen(8000);
var socketio = io.listen(server);
```

If you have some experience with Node.js or Socket.IO, this code is pretty straightforward. What we're basically doing is setting up an HTTP server, specifying how it will reply to requests, making it listen on a port (in this case, we're going to listen on port 8000), and attaching Socket.IO to it so that it can automatically serve the Socket.IO JavaScript files and set up the websocket functionality.

Now we set up the small bits of Redis code to support our functionality. The Redis client we set up with Node.js must subscribe to a specific chat channel, and deal with messages on that channel when they arrive. So that's what we do next:

```
// if the Redis server emits a connect event, it means we're ready to work,
// which in turn means we should subscribe to our channels. Which we will.
rc.on("connect", function() {
  rc.subscribe("chat");  // we could subscribe to more channels here
  });
// When we get a message in one of the channels we're subscribed to,
 // we send it over to all connected clients.
 rc.on("message", function (channel, message) {
    console.log("Sending: " + message);
    socketio.sockets.emit('message', message); })
```

As you can see, our actual Redis code is extremely simple. All we do is listen for messages on a specific channel, and when they arrive, we broadcast them to all clients that are connected to us.

Implementing the client side code

With the server side part completed, all we have to do is create a small page that connects to Node.js, sets up Socket.IO on the client side, and then deals with incoming and outgoing messages. So let's create a page like that now. Here's the main trunk for a very simple HTML5 page:

```
<!doctype html><html lang="en">
  <head>
    <meta charset="utf-8">
    <title>Chat with Redis</title>
  </head>
  <body>
    <ul id="messages">
      <!-- chat messages go here -->
    </ul>
  </body>
</html>
```

Now we need to include the two main pieces we need to get the functionality working: jQuery and Socket.IO. We'll grab the first from Google's CDN, and the second from our Node.js server (Socket.IO takes care of setting this up for you automatically). Insert these two lines in the head section of your page:

```
<script src="https://ajax.googleapis.com/ajax/libs/jquery/1.6.1/jquery.min.js">
  </script>
<script src="http://localhost:8000/socket.io/socket.io.js">
</script>
```

We're now ready to connect to Node.js from this page and start listening to and processing messages. Add the following code to your head section:

```
<script>
  var socket = io.connect('localhost', { port: 8000 });

  socket.on('message', function(data){
    var li = new Element('li').insert(data);
    $('messages').insert({top: li});
  }
</script>
```

This piece of JavaScript makes the client-side Socket.IO connect to our Node.js instance on port 8000 and start listening to message events. When a message arrives, it creates a new list element and adds it to the unordered list we had already added to our code. Remember, this is very simple code and the resulting chat page will look ugly by default, but it is also trivial to update it to look better.

All we're missing at this point is a form and a way to send messages from one client to the server so that they can be broadcast to everyone else. This is done with Socket.IO's emit function, which we already used on the server side as well. Write something like:

```
<form id="chatform" action="">
  <input id="chattext" type="text" value="" />
  <input type="submit" value="Send" />
</form>
```

```
<script>
  $('#chatform').submit(function() {
    socket.emit('message', $('chattext').val());
    $('chattext').val(""); // cleanup the field
    return false;
  });
</script>
```

When a client fills the form and clicks Send, jQuery will use our `socket` variable to emit a message event to the server, which will then broadcast the message to everyone else. The `return false` statement in the last script tag keeps the form from actually being submitted. Our submission code is handled by Socket.IO.

Further improvements

In the previous sections, we built the main pieces of a chat system using Node.js, Socket.IO, and Redis. There are many ways we could improve our code. Instead of sending and receiving regular strings, we could create small JSON snippets that include, with the message, a bit of metadata like a username or avatar. We could also improve our server-side code to include multiple channels, or allow subscribing to several channels using a pattern. The possibilities are endless, and Redis's pub/sub implementation makes it trivial to implement robust solutions for chat or notifications.

3.5. Implementing an Inverted-Index Text Search with Redis

Problem

An inverted index is an index data structure that stores mappings of words (or other content) to their locations in a file, document, database, etc. This is generally used to implement full text search, but it requires previous indexing of the documents to be searched.

In this recipe, we'll use Redis as the storage backend for a full-text search implementation.

Solution

Our implementation will use one set per word, containing document IDs. In order to allow fast searches, we'll index all the documents beforehand. Search itself is performed by splitting the query into words and intersecting the matching sets. This will return the IDs of the documents containing all the words we search for.[1]

---

1. This recipe is based on an example by Salvatore Sanfilippo (*https://gist.github.com/120067*) released under the BSD license.

Discussion

Indexing

Let's say we have a hundred documents or web pages that we want to allows searches on. The first step is indexing these. In order to do so, we should split the text into its separate words and perhaps exclude stop words (*http://bit.ly/stop_words*) and words under three characters in length. We'll use a Ruby script to do this:

```ruby
def id_for_document(filename)
  doc_id = $redis.hget("documents", filename)
  if doc_id.nil?
    doc_id = $redis.incr("next_document_id")
    $redis.hset("documents", filename, doc_id)
    $redis.hset("filenames", doc_id, filename)
  end
  doc_id
end

STOP_WORDS = ["the", "of", "to", "and", "a", "in", "is", "it", "you", "that"]
f = File.open(filename)
doc_id = id_for_document(filename)
f.each_line do |l|
  l.strip.split(/ |,|\)|\(|\;|\./).each do |word|
    continue if word.size <= 3 || STOP_WORDS.include?(word)
    add_word(word, doc_id)
  end
end
```

So, we've filtered the words that will be added to the index and generated unique IDs for our documents. We still need the indexing function:

```ruby
def add_word(word, doc_id)
  $redis.sadd("word:#{word}", doc_id)
end
```

So, for each each word that we find in our documents, we have created a new set containing the IDs of the documents where that word can be found.

Searching

The advantage of inverted indexes is that search is really fast since most of the work is done during the indexing of the document. In order to search, we only need to intersect the sets of the words in our search query. The following code uses the redis-rb interface to Redis to execute commands against the Redis server in our Ruby client program.

```ruby
def search(*terms)
  document_ids = $redis.sinter(*terms.map{|t| "word:#{t}"})
  $redis.hmget("filenames", *document_ids)
end
```

SINTER *set1 set2* .. (*http://redis.io/commands/sinter*) intersects a given number of sets.

Scoring

The previous approach is somewhat limited and very simple, but easily extendable. One thing we could do is rank our documents so that when returning search results, we take a score under consideration: a higher score meaning more revelance (such as if a word is in the subject or title of the document) or simply higher frequency. Let's change the indexing function to the following:

```
def add_word(word, doc_id)
  $redis.zincrby("word:#{word}", 1, doc_id)
end
```

Searching becomes a bit more complicated:

```
def search(*terms)
  document_ids = $redis.multi do
    $redis.zinterstore("temp_set", terms.map{|t| "word:#{t}"})
    $redis.zrevrange("temp_set", 0, -1)
  end.last
  $redis.hmget("filenames", *document_ids)
end
```

Notice the use of a `multi` function in the previous code. This is because we have a potential race condition in the `temp_set` sorted set. Whenever you have two or more commands that must both be applied before anyone else tries to access the data they change (as we do here with `ZINTERSTORE` followed by `ZREVRANGE`), the potential for a race condition exists.

In order to avoid running into this race condition, while performing parallel search queries, we must either use Redis's `MULTI/EXEC` commands or be able to generate a unique key for each search query. (In that case, we should also clean up after ourselves and delete the temporary sorted set).

The `MULTI` (*http://redis.io/commands/multi*) and `EXEC` (*http://redis.io/commands/exec*) commands allow transactional behavior in Redis (*http://redis.io/topics/transactions*). All commands written in a `MULTI/EXEC` block are assured to be run sequentially, which means that no other Redis client gets served during the length of the block. In the previous example, it eliminates the race condition in `temp_set` because other clients are unable to change the value between the `ZINTERSTORE` and `ZREVRANGE` operations. Using `DISCARD` (*http://redis.io/commands/discard*) inside a transaction will abort the transaction, discarding all the commands and return to the normal state.

Since the commands are processed only after EXEC is called, only at that moment will you receive the replies for all the commands inside the transaction. Therefore it's impossible to use the response of a command run inside the transaction within the same transaction. In order to achieve that, you'll need to use WATCH (*http://redis.io/commands/watch*).

redis-rb has no explicit EXEC call. Instead, the beginning and end of the block submitted to your *multi* function mark the beginning and end of the transaction. At the end of your block, redis-rb internally calls EXEC.

Quick Reference for Inverted-Index Algorithm

ZINCRBY `zset-name increment element` (*http://redis.io/commands/zincrby*)
> Adds or increments the score of an element in a sorted set. As with ZADD and SADD, the set will be created if it doesn't exist.

ZINTERSTORE `destination-zset number-of-zsets-to-intersect zset1 [zset2 ...]` [WEIGHTS `weight1 [weight2 ...]`] [AGGREGATE SUM | MIN | MAX] (*http://redis.io/commands/zinterstore*)
> Gets the intersection of a given number of ZSETS and store the result in a new ZSET. It's also possible to pass along a muliplication factor for each ZSET (WEIGHTS) or to specify the aggregation function. By default, it's a sum of the scores in all the sets, but it can also be the maximum or minimum value.

ZREVRANGE `zset-name start-index stop-index` [WITHSCORES] (*http://redis.io/commands/zrevrange*)
> Returns the elements in the sorted set within the given range, in descending order. The command can also optionally include the scores of the elements in the returned result. The ZRANGE (*http://redis.io/commands/zrange*) command performs the same operation, but in ascending order.

Other improvements

There are many improvements that could be done for this search implementation:

Case sensitivity
> We could make this example case-insensitive by downcasing (or upcasing) the words before indexing and the search terms before querying.

Fuzzy searching
> You might also be interested in implementing fuzzy searching as part of your search application. It consists basically of taking common misspellings into consideration. In our example, this would be done at the indexing phase by indexing the terms along with the misspellings, either retrieved from a list or by using a specific

algorithm for that purpose (for example, a phonetic (*http://en.wikipedia.org/wiki/Phonetic_algorithm*) one).

Partial word matching

This can be very useful, but will also increase the memory usage of your index and possibly give you many unwanted search results. In order to achieve this, you'd have to decompose your words into substrings and index those. For example, to index the word *matching*, you'd have to add all of these:

> matching
> mat
> matc
> match
> matchi
> matchin

And that's assuming that you've set a minimum length of three characters and that you'd always match at least the beginning of the word. If you're interested in all the possible combinations, you'd need to index many other substrings of that word.

The use of sorted sets is useful for both this and the previous enhancement (fuzzy searching). You could leverage them to give lower scores to partial words (perhaps proportional to the length of the word) and to the misspellings in order to improve the quality of your search results.

INCR *key (http://redis.io/commands/incr)*
> Increments the integer stored at *key* by 1.

INCRBY *key value (http://redis.io/commands/incrby)*
> Performs the same operation as INCR, but incrementing by *value* instead.

DECR *key (http://redis.io/commands/decr)*
> Decrements the integer stored at *key* by 1.

DECRBY *key value (http://redis.io/commands/decrby)*
> Performs the same operation as DECR, but decrementing by *value* instead.

3.6. Analytics and Time-Based Data

Problem

Storing analytics or other time-based data poses somewhat of a challenge for traditional storage systems (like an RDBMS). Perhaps you want to do rate limiting on incoming traffic (which requires fast and highly concurrent updates) or simply track visitors (or more complex metrics) to your website and plot them on a chart.

While there are many ways of storing this kind of data in other systems, Redis is a perfect candidate due to its powerful data structures.

Solution

Redis is ideally suited for storing this type of data, and for tracking events in particular. The atomic and fast (in O(1) time) HINCR and HINCRBY commands, combined with fast data look-ups, make it a good fit.

A good and memory-efficient way of storing this data in Redis is to use hashes to store the counters, increment them using HINCRBY, and then fetch them using HGET and HMGET. Finding the top elements is also easily achieved using the SORT command.

Discussion

For simplicity's sake, in this example, we'll track only hits. This could easily be extended to track any kind of events.

```
require 'rubygems'
require 'active_support/time'

def add_hit(id)
  $redis.sadd("clients", id)
  $redis.hincrby("stats/client:#{id}", "total", 1)
  $redis.hincrby("stats/client:#{id}", Date.today.to_s(:number), 1)
end
```

What we're doing here is adding the ID for this user (which could be simply an IP address, if we're tracking visitors to a website) to a list of clients (or visitors) and then logging hits in two different time slots: a "total" and a daily one. This allows us to track hits per day and globally over time.

```
def hits(id, day = Date.today)
  $redis.hget("stats/client:#{id}", day.to_s(:number)).to_i
end

def over_limit?(id, limit)
  hits(id) > limit
end
```

This also allows us to enforce rate limiting by simply checking whether that client has gone over the limit for a given time period.

Fetching data for a given period of time is also a trivial and efficient operation that can be used to plot a chart or display the data in some other way:

```
def keys(beg_p, end_p)
  keys = []
  while beg_p <= end_p
    keys << if block_given?
```

```
      yield(beg_p.to_s(:number))
    else
      beg_p.to_s(:number)
    end
    beg_p += 1.day
  end

  keys
end

def stats_for_period(id, beginning_of_period, end_of_period)
  beg_p = Date.parse(beginning_of_period)
  end_p = Date.parse(end_of_period)

  $redis.hmget "stats/client:#{id}", *keys(beg_p, end_p)
end
```

We can also fetch the top clients for any "time slot" that we're storing data for, using the SORT command. SORT allows us to sort a set, sorted set, or list—in our case, the `cli ents` set—optionally using external keys—our time slots—while specifying order, offset, limit, etc.:

```
def top_clients(period = "total", limit = 5)
  $redis.sort("clients", :by => "stats/client:*->#{period}", :order => "DESC",
              :get => ["#", "stats/client:*->#{period}"],
              :limit => [0, limit])
end
```

This implementation, using hashes, is highly optimized for storage, retrieval, and updating (all O(1) operations) but not for calculating the top users (particularly for a date range). Should you require those operations—for example, when displaying a high-score table—you can reimplement the sort using sorted sets, which guarantee that you get your data sorted:

```
def add_hit(id)
  $redis.zincrby("stats/total", 1, id)
  $redis.zincrby("stats/#{Date.today.to_s(:number)}", 1, id)
end

def hits(id, day = Date.today)
  $redis.zrank("stats/#{day.to_s(:number)}", id)
end

def over_limit?(id, limit)
  hits(id) > limit
end

def stats_for_period(id, beginning_of_period, end_of_period)
  beg_p = Date.parse(beginning_of_period)
  end_p = Date.parse(end_of_period)

  keys(beg_p, end_p) { |k| $redis.zrank("stats/#{k}", id) }
```

```ruby
end

def top_clients(period = "total", limit = 5)
  $redis.zrevrange("stats/#{period}", 0, limit, :withscores => true)
end

def top_for_period(beginning_of_period, end_of_period, limit = 5)
  beg_p = Date.parse(beginning_of_period)
  end_p = Date.parse(end_of_period)

  result_key = "top/#{beg_p.to_s(:number)}/#{end_p.to_s(:number)}"
  if $redis.exists(result_key)

    return $redis.zrevrange(result_key, 0, limit, :withscores => true)
  end

  $redis.multi do
    $redis.zunionstore result_key, keys(beg_p, end_p){|k| "stats/#{k}"}
    $redis.expire result_key, 10.minutes
    $redis.zrevrange result_key, 0, limit, :withscores => true
  end.last
end
```

Notice that we're keeping the result of ZUNIONSTORE and setting an expiration timestamp on it. That's a common Redis pattern: caching the result of a computationally expensive operation and, upon request, checking the cache before redoing the operation.

In the previous example, where we're using hashes, we could also store the result of SORT (using the STORE option) and then check for its existence in a similar way with EXISTS.

This particular example has a race condition: if the cache doesn't exist, we might end up doing the ZUNIONSTORE several times. Since the expected output is the same or a more updated one, it might be better to live with the race condition than to use WATCH and lock other clients while we're doing client side calculations (in this case, generating the keys).

When using sorted sets, these top operations are much more efficient (because the data is already ordered) but your memory usage will be higher.

Quick Reference for Analytics Techniques

HINCRBY *hash-name field increment-value* *(http://redis.io/commands/hincrby)*
> Increments an integer stored in a hash by *increment-value*. This command is similar to INCRBY, but instead of increment strings, it's used in hashes. The *increment-value* can also be negative.

HMGET *hash-name field1 [field2 ...]* *(http://redis.io/commands/hmget)*
> Fetches several fields from a given hash. This command is similar to HGET, but allows you to get several fields in a single operation.

SORT *key* [BY *pattern*] [LIMIT *offset count*] [GET *pattern1* [GET *pattern2 ...*]]
[ASC|DESC] [ALPHA] [STORE *destination*] *(http://redis.io/commands/sort)*
> Allows you to sort a list, set, or sorted set, comparing their values as numbers (if ALPHA is specified, values are assumed to be strings). The sorting can also be done using "external" keys, queried using a pattern from individual strings or hashes, as in our previous example where we did:
>
> ```
> SORT clients BY stats/client:*->20110407
> ```
>
> The wildcard * is replaced with the members of the set, so the sorting is done based on the values matching the field 20110407 in those hashtables. If we're storing the analytics data in strings instead of hashtables, we would omit ->:
>
> ```
> SORT clients BY stats/client:*/20110407
> ```
>
> Using the same patterns, you can also get more data (for example, the values you used for sorting) in addition to the sorted list. Optionally, the output of SORT can be stored in a list instead of returned. Please refer to the Redis documentation for some examples.

ZRANK *set-name member* *(http://redis.io/commands/zrank)*
> Returns the rank (index) of the given member in the sorted set.

ZUNIONSTORE *destination number-of-keys sorted-set1 [sorted-set2 ...]* [WEIGHTS
weight1 [weight2 ...]]] [AGGREGATE SUM|MIN|MAX] *(http://redis.io/commands/zunionstore)*
> Aggregates a collection of sorted sets and stores it as a new sorted set at destination. Optionally, you can specify weights (a multiplication factor) per set and the aggregation function: sum (the default), maximum scores, or minimum scores.

EXISTS *key* *(http://redis.io/commands/exists)*
> Checks for the existence of a key. Returns 1 i the key exists, and 0 if it does not.

3.7. Implementing a Job Queue with Redis

Problem

A typical use case for Redis has been a queue. Although this is owed mostly to Resque (*http://bit.ly/resque_intro*) (a project started by Github after trying all the other Ruby job queueing solutions). In fact, there are several other implementations (*http://bit.ly/ emerging_usecase*) (Barbershop (*http://bit.ly/with_Barbershop*), qr (*https://github.com/ tnm/qr*), presque (*http://bit.ly/with_presque*)) and tutorials ("Creating Processing Queues with Redis" (*http://bit.ly/how-to-queues*)). Nevertheless, it's interesting in the context of this book to give an example implementation (inspired by existing ones).

Solution

Let's implement our queues on top of lists, which provide atomic push/pop operations and have constant access time to the list's head and tail. We'll also keep a set that lists all the existing queues for introspection purposes. Since sets assure uniqueness, we don't need to worry whether our queue already exists in the set.

Discussion

Enqueueing

Let's begin with enqueueing. In order to do so, we need only to RPUSH into a key that is either nil or contains a list. Redis lists contain strings, so we must serialize our data. In this case, we opted for JSON.

```
def enqueue(queue_name, data)
  $redis.sadd("queues", queue_name)
  $redis.rpush("queue:#{queue_name}", data.to_json)
end
```

Let's also write some auxiliary functions for such operations as emptying a queue, removing it, checking its length, removing a job, and peeking into the queue to check what the next job is:

```
def clear(queue_name)
  $redis.del("queue:#{queue_name}")
end

def destroy(queue_name)
  self.clear(queue_name)
  $redis.srem("queues", "queue:#{queue_name}")
end

def length(queue_name)
  $redis.llen("queue:#{queue_name}")
end
```

```
def remove_job(queue_name, data)
  $redis.lrem("queue:#{queue_name}", 0, data.to_json)
end

def peek(queue_name)
  $redis.lrange("queue:#{queue_name}", 0, 0)
end
```

Notice how we just delete the list (instead of using LTRIM) from Redis when emptying the queue. This isn't a problem as Redis treats a nonexisting value as an empty queue. In fact, using the length function after emptying the queue with del will return 0.

Beware that removing a single element from a list isn't cheap. Because lists are optimized for head and tail access, in order to remove an element from the middle of the list, Redis will have to iterate through it. You also need to know the exact value that you want to remove—you can't apply regular expressions or other matchers and you can't remove by index.

Quick Reference for Additions to Lists

When dealing with indexes, the head of the list is element 0. When counting from the end, -1 refers to the last element, -2 to the next-to-last, etc.

RPUSH *list-name value (http://redis.io/commands/rpush)*
Inserts the given value at the tail of the list-name list. Should this list be nil, it will be created.

LPUSH *list-name value (http://redis.io/commands/lpush)*
Like RPUSH, but inserts the element at the head o f the list.

LRANGE *list-name start-index stop-index (http://redis.io/commands/lrange)*
Returns the list elements in the specified range (including the rightmost element specified).

LTRIM *list-name start-index stop-index (http://redis.io/commands/ltrim)*
Trims the list so that it only contains the elements in the specified range. It's similar to the LRANGE command, but instead of just returning the elements, it trims the list.

LLEN *list-name (http://redis.io/commands/llen)*
Returns the length of the given list.

LREM *list-name count value (http://redis.io/commands/lrem)*
Removes *count* occurrences of *value* from the list. If *count* is positive, the elements are removed starting from the head, if it's negative, they are removed starting from the tail, and if it's 0, all occurrences of *value* are removed.

Dequeueing

Our queue workers are now ready to start consuming the jobs. In order to dequeue jobs from the queue, we can pop them one a time:

```
def dequeue(queue_name)
  $redis.lpop("queue:#{queue_name}")
end
```

This previous approach has a problem, though: if there are no jobs in the queue, nothing will be returned and we need to check again later. However, if we check too often, we're consuming both Redis and worker resources, and if we don't check every few seconds we add latency to our job processing. To resolve this problem, Redis offers a blocking pop operation.

```
def dequeue(queue_name)
  $redis.blpop("queue:#{queue_name}", 60)
end
```

BLPOP (*http://redis.io/commands/blpop*) is a blocking POP operation. If the list is empty, it blocks for up to the number of seconds specified in the second argument, waiting for an element to be put on the list. By reimplementing the dequeue method using a blocking pop, we solve that issue. Our worker will be blocked on that method call until there is an element in the queue, at which point it returns. We can also set a timeout for this operation so that, for example, it returns after 60 seconds if no job is put on the queue.

```
def work(queue_name)
  while true do
    job = self.dequeue(queue_name)
    process_job(job) unless job.nil?
  end
end
```

 If you're not a using a blocking implementation, you should add a "sleep" at the end of the loop. Otherwise you'll end up using all your CPU checking for jobs in an empty queue (assuming you're not filling it up quickly enough).

Implementing our job processing functionality is easy enough by just dequeuing and processing jobs in a loop. What if we want to have multiple queues, representing higher and lower priority jobs? Luckily, BLPOP supports multiple lists. (LPOP and RPOP work on only one list.) People familiar with Unix and Linux system programming can see a resemblance to the *select*(2) call, which simultaneously monitors several file handles for activity.

```
def dequeue(queues)
  $redis.blpop(*queues.map{|q| "queue:#{q}"}.push(60))
end
```

```
def work(queues)
  while true do
    job = self.dequeue(queues)
    process_job(job) unless job.nil?
  end
end

work(['higher-priority', 'high-priority'])
```

The relevant change here is the way BLPOP is used. If passed multiple lists, it will block waiting to return elements from the specified lists, using their order in its argument list as the priority. In our example, if there are jobs in both the first list and the second list in queues, the job from the first list will be returned first. Because queues are stored in our queues set, we can start our workers without explicitly knowing the queue names.

```
work($redis.smembers("queues").map{|q| "queue:#{q}"})
```

Beware that this won't respect the order of your queues because we're simply grabbing the set from Redis (with no order specified). To treat the queues in a priority order, you'd need to use a sorted set and assign different scores to your queues.

Quick Reference for Removals from Lists

LPOP *list-name (http://redis.io/commands/lpop)*
    Removes and returns the element at the head of the list.

RPOP *list-name (http://redis.io/commands/lpop)*
    Like LPOP, but performs the action at the tail of the list.

BLPOP *list-name1 [list-name2 ...] timeout-value (http://redis.io/commands/blpop)*
    A blocking POP operation. It returns when any list has an element. If multiple lists have elements, *list-name1* takes precedence over *list-name2*, and so forth.

BRPOP *list-name1 list-name2 ... timeout-value (http://redis.io/commands/blpop)*
    Like BLPOP, but performs the action at the tails of the lists.

 Although using lists is the most common way to implement queues in Redis, you can also achieve similar behavior by using sets and the commands SADD and SPOP if the order in which the commands are executed is unimportant in your particular case. However, this has many disadvantages: added overhead (sets usually require more memory) and no blocking functions. There is at least one case where using sets over lists could be an advantage: if your jobs are very heavy (slow or expensive in terms of resources) and you're bound to have many duplicated jobs. The guarantee of uniqueness might be a decisive factor for you to choose sets.

3.8. Extending Redis

Problem

While the Redis source is very readable and easily modifiable, you might find yourself in need of an easier way to tweak or extend Redis. Perhaps you'd like a new command or simply to modify the return value of an existing one. You might also be interested in reducing the amount of traffic (and therefore latency) between your application and Redis while performing a large number of operations.

Solution

In Redis 2.6, and after being widely requested by its users, *scripting* was introduced. This was achieved by integrating the Redis server with the Lua C API.

Lua (*http://www.lua.org/*) is a language that is often embedded into applications in order to provide scripting functionality. The simplicity of Lua's (and its C API's) makes it a great, light-weight, simple fit for Redis. Since Redis runs mostly as a single-threaded process, these scripts should be as efficient as possible; otherwise they'll block other clients from using the Redis server.

Discussion

The scripting functionality consists of two simple commands: EVAL and EVALSHA, the latter being used only to reduce bandwidth.

```
require 'rubygems'
require 'redis'

$redis = Redis.new
increxby = <<LUA
  if redis.call("exists",KEYS[1]) == 1
    then
      return redis.call("incrby",KEYS[1], ARGV[1])
    else
      return nil
    end
LUA

$redis.eval(increxby,[:counter], [1])
```

The previous example (inspired by Salvatore Sanfilippo's scripting release blog post (*http://bit.ly/Sanfilippo*)) implements a conditional increment functionality (the condition being the previous existence of the key). This code is not only readable but should also perform very well. In addition, the Lua scripts are executed atomically, so you can use them in same way you'd use MULTI / EXEC but keep in mind that script execution blocks your Redis server, so beware of slow scripts. Previously, the way to achieve this (using a more direct approach such as the redis-rb API we've used in this chapter) would be:

```
$redis.watch(:counter)
if $redis.exists(:counter)
  $redis.multi do
    $redis.incrby(:counter, 1)
  end
else
  $redis.unwatch
end
```

This implementation has an issue, however, because the client has to send at least three separate operations to the server (WATCH, EXISTS, and the transaction block) as opposed to the atomic EVAL. First, it might fail to increment the counter if there are concurrent operations, because the counter key is modified which causes the transaction to abort. And the three operations will most likely be slower.

However, depending on the length of your script, you might end up using a lot of bandwith, as the scripts are not stored by the server and have to be sent along in every call. Enter EVALSHA:

```
require 'digest/sha1'
def eval_script(body, keys, arguments)
  $redis.evalsha(Digest::SHA1.hexdigest(body), keys, arguments)
rescue Redis::CommandError
  $redis.eval(body, keys, arguments)
end
```

This command allows us to reuse previously loaded scripts by sending their SHA1 hash instead of their body. If the Redis server hasn't seen this script before, it will return an error and you can use EVAL to load it instead.

In order to manage your Lua scripts, Redis provides a few more commands that allow you to check for their existence, remove them from the cache, halt their execution, or load them without executing.

When reading the argument list for the EVAL and EVALSHA commands, you might have noticed that keys and arguments are passed differently even though there's no apparent reason to do so. This will allow Redis Cluster (which is not yet released, but you can try it out in the unstable branch of the official repository) to forward that command to the server containing the given keys. At the moment, this rule is not enforced, so you can hardcode the used keys in your scripts or pass them as arguments, but keep in mind that your code will most likely not be compatible with the future Redis Cluster.

3.9. Manipulating Compressed Data

Problem

Given that Redis keeps all of its data in memory, you might be considering compressing in order to reduce your hardware requirements. However, you would like to retain the ability to perform a few operations on the server.

Solution

Along with the introduction of Lua scripting, Redis bundles a few libraries, including a MessagePack implementation. MessagePack is a data interchange format (like JSON or XML) that allows you to represent some data structures like arrays or hashtables in a compact form. By storing your data in MessagePack inside your Redis server, you reduce your memory consumption while retaining the ability to manipulate it server-side.

Discussion

Like most things in Redis, using MessagePack is quite simple, provided you read the previous chapter on scripting.

The entire API of the lua-cmsgpack library is composed of two functions: pack and unpack.

Let's implement something like HINCRBY and some other helper functions like HGET on top of the lua-cmsgpack library.

```
module MsgPack
  HSET_BODY = <<LUA
    local dict = {}
    local packed = redis.call("get", KEYS[1])
    if packed then
      dict = cmsgpack.unpack(packed)
    end
    dict[ARGV[1]] = ARGV[2]
    redis.call("set", KEYS[1], cmsgpack.pack(dict))
LUA

  HGET_BODY = <<LUA
    local packed = redis.call("get", KEYS[1])
    if packed then
      return cmsgpack.unpack(packed)[ARGV[1]]
    end
LUA

  HINCRBY_BODY = <<LUA
    local dict = {}
    local packed = redis.call("get", KEYS[1])
    if packed then
      dict = cmsgpack.unpack(packed)
    end
    dict[ARGV[1]] = (dict[ARGV[1]] or 0)  + ARGV[2]
    redis.call("set", KEYS[1], cmsgpack.pack(dict))
    return dict[ARGV[1]]
LUA

  def self.hset(hash_name, key, value)
    $r.eval(HSET_BODY, [hash_name], [key,value])
  end

  def self.hget(hash_name, key)
    $r.eval(HGET_BODY, [hash_name], [key])
  end

  def self.hincrby(hash_name, key, increment=1)
    $r.eval(HINCRBY_BODY, [hash_name], [key, increment])
  end
end
```

Obviously, this implementation, while clear and readable, won't perform as well as the Redis native Hash implementation (and that also has an impact on concurrency) but it would allow you to have very compact hashes. Redis also includes a JSON Lua library, so you could have the server convert `MessagePack` to `JSON` (or the other way around) if you use `JSON` in your application.

You can read more about Redis scripting in the documentation (*http://www.redis.io/ commands/eval*). To learn more about Lua, read the Lua tutorials (*http://lua-users.org/ wiki/LuaTutorial*).

CHAPTER 4

Redis Administration and Maintenance

In this chapter, we'll try to focus on recipes related to operating Redis servers, instead of programming applications or data modeling. These tasks vary widely, but include starting a Redis slave, upgrading an existing server, performing backups, sharding, and handling a dataset larger than your available memory.

4.1. Configuring Persistence

Problem

One of the advantages of Redis over other key/value stores like memcached is its support for persistence—in fact, it even comes preconfigured with this support. This functionality enables you to perform some operations that wouldn't be possible otherwise, like upgrading your server without down time or performing backups.

Nevertheless, persistence should be configured in a way that suits your dataset and usage patterns.

Solution

The default persistence model is *snapshotting*, which consists of saving the entire database to disk in the RDB format (basically a compressed database dump). This can be done periodically at set times, or every time a configurable number of keys changes.

The alternative is using an Append Only File (AOF). This might be a better option if you have a large dataset or your data doesn't change very frequently.

Discussion

Snapshotting

As previously stated, snapshotting is the default persistence mode for Redis. It asynchronously performs a full dump of your database to disk, overwriting the previous dump only if successful. Therefore, the latest dump should always be in your *dbfile name* location.

You can configure snapshotting using `save seconds keys-changed` statements in your configuration file, in the following format:

```
save seconds keys-changed
```

The snapshot will occur when both conditions match. A typical example that ensures that all your data is saved every few minutes is: `save 600 1` which will perform a snapshot every 10 minutes if any key in your server has changed.

You can manually trigger snapshotting with the `SAVE` and `BGSAVE` commands. `BGSAVE` (*http://redis.io/commands/bgsave*) forks the main Redis process and saves the DB to disk in the background. Redis executes this operation itself if you have SAVE statements in your configuration file. SAVE (*http://redis.io/commands/save*) performs the same operation as `BGSAVE` but does so in the foreground, thereby blocking your Redis server.

If you come to the conclusion that snapshotting is putting too much strain on your Redis servers you might want to consider using slaves for persistence (by commenting out all the `save` statements in your masters and enabling them only on the slaves), or using AOF instead. In particular, if you have a big dataset or a dataset that doesn't change often, consider using AOF.

AOF

The `Append Only File` persistence mode keeps a log of the commands that change your dataset in a separate file. Like most writes on modern operating systems, any data logged to AOF is left in memory buffers and written to disk at intervals of a few seconds using the system's `fsync` call. You can configure how often the AOF gets synched to disk by putting `appendfsync` statements in your configuration file. Valid options are `always`, `everysec`, and `no`.

 Disabling `fsync` is not safe, as it leaves the decision to your operating system about when to actually write the data to disk.

AOF can be used together with snapshotting. But you might decide to suppress snapshots because they put too much load on your server. If you're not snapshotting, be sure to write the AOF to a RAID array or have at least one Redis slave that you can recover data from in case of disaster.

 BGREWRITEAOF (*http://redis.io/commands/bgrewriteaof*) rewrites the AOF to match the current database. Depending on how often you update existing data, this will greatly reduce the size of the AOF. Since Redis 2.4, BGREWRITEAOF is run automatically. Nevertheless, should you wish to, you can also run it manually. The rewrite is done in the background, so as to not block your Redis server.

4.2. Starting a Redis Slave

Problem

Database slaves are useful for a number of reasons. You might need them to load-balance your queries, keep hot standby servers, perform maintenance operations, or simply inspect your data.

Solution

Redis supports *master-slave* replication natively: you can have multiple slaves per master and slaves connecting to slaves. You can configure replication on the configuration file before starting a server or by connecting to a running server and using the SLAVEOF command.

Discussion

In order to configure a Redis slave using the configuration file, you should add the following to your *redis.conf*:

```
slaveof master-ip-or-hostname masterport
```

Start or restart the server afterwards. Should your Redis master have password authentication enabled, you'll need to specify it as well:

```
masterauth master-password
```

If you want to turn a running Redis server into a slave (or switch to a different master), you can do it using the SLAVEOF (*http://redis.io/commands/slaveof*) command:

```
SLAVEOF master-ip-or-hostname [masterport]
```

As in the previous example, if you're using authentication, you'll need to specify it beforehand:

```
CONFIG SET masterauth password
```

Keep in mind that should your server restart, this configuration will be lost. Therefore, you should also commit your changes to the configuration file.

 CONFIG SET (*http://redis.io/commands/config-set*) allows you to read configuration parameters from a running Redis server. CONFIG GET (*http://redis.io/commands/config-get*) enables you to set configuration parameters on a running Redis server. Please refer to the documentation for these commands' parameters.

4.3. Using Redis As a Memcache Replacement

Problem

Memcache is a widely used, high-performance distributed caching system, providing a simple, lightweight, in-memory key value store. Given that Redis supports all of Memcache's features, you can in fact use Redis instead of Memcache in your caching infrastructure and at the same time take advantage of some of the extra features available in Redis.

Solution

Our solution for this problem focuses on configuring Redis to match two of the major differences it has from memcache: persistence and maximum memory usage. Because Memcache doesn't support any kind of persistence, we'll disable it in Redis, and configure the maximum amount of memory used by Redis (a mandatory setting in memcache).

Discussion

In a previous chapter we explained how to configure the different persistence modes in Redis, but we didn't explain how to disable them. The answer is simple, though: just remove all the save statements from your *redis.conf* and set appendfsync to no. Keep in mind that if you haven't configured persistence, it's probably enabled, because it's the default setting.

When it comes to maximum memory usage, Redis allows you to configure both the amount of memory and the eviction policy used when the limit is reached. The amount is quite straightforward: adding maxmemory 1g to your configuration specifies a maximum memory usage of 1 gigabyte. The maxmemory-policy setting has six different policies, which determine what action is taken once the memory limit is hit:

volatile-lru

> Removes a volatile key (one that has expiration set) using an LRU (*http://en.wiki pedia.org/wiki/Cache_algorithms#Least_Recently_Used*) (least recently used) algorithm.

allkeys-lru

> Removes a key from the database using an LRU algorithm.

volatile-random

> Removes a volatile key at random from the database.

allkeys-random

> Removes a random key from the database.

volatile-ttl

> Removes the key with the lowest TTL (closer to expiration).

noeviction

> Disables eviction. Write operations to the database will raise an error if they'd exceed the maxmemory setting.

As with any other Redis configuration variable, these can be set programatically using CONFIG SET.

4.4. Upgrading Redis

Problem

At some point in the life of your system you might need to upgrade Redis. Unfortunately, Redis can't do online binary upgrades, and doing a server restart means that your application won't be able to talk to Redis for a (possibly long) period of time. But that doesn't mean that there aren't other ways to achieve it without incurring downtime. You might also want to move your current Redis database to another system for maintenance purposes, a hardware upgrade, etc.

Solution

Our solution will involve starting a new Redis server in slave mode, switching over the clients to the slave and promoting the new server to the master role. To make the example easier to understand, let's assume we have a Redis server listening on port 6379.

> It might be easier to start the slave on a new server than on the existing one. This is because of memory requirements, and because you can reuse the same configuration file, directories, and port for the slave, changing only the hostname or IP address.

1. Install the new Redis version without restarting your existing server.

2. Create a new *redis.conf*, specifying that Redis runs on port 6380 (assuming you're on the same system—if you're not, you can still use 6379 or any other available port) and a different DB directory (you don't want to have 2 Redis servers reading or writing the same files).

3. Start the new server.

4. Connect to the new server and issue the command:

    ```
    SLAVEOF localhost 6379
    ```

    This will trigger a BGSAVE on the master server, and upon completion the new (slave) server will start replicating. You can check the current status using the INFO command on the slave. When you see master_link_status:up, the replication is active.

5. Since your new Redis server is now up-to-date, you can start moving over your clients to this new server. You can verify the number of clients connected to a server with the INFO command; check the connected_clients variable.

6. When all your clients are connected to the slave server, you still have two tasks to complete: disable the replication and shut down the master server.

 INFO (*http://redis.io/commands/info*) returns information about the server including replication status, uptime, memory usage, number of keys per database and other statistics.

1. Connect to the slave server and issue:

    ```
    SLAVEOF NO ONE
    ```

    This will stop replication and effectively promote your slave to a master. This is important, because master servers are responsible for sending expirations to their slaves.

2. Now connect to your old master server and issue:

    ```
    SHUTDOWN
    ```

    The old master server will perform a SAVE and shutdown.

3. Your new Redis system is up and running, but make sure that all your configuration files, init scripts, backups, etc., are pointing to the right location and starting the correct server. It's easy to forget those routine operations, but you should, at the very least, certify that nothing wrong will happen in case of a server restart.

Discussion

Doing an online upgrade has a couple of (possibly steep) requirements: you need to able to point your Redis clients to another server, either by use of a proxy, by having failover built-in to your clients (so that they connect to a different server once you bring the master down), or just by simply tell them to connect to another server. You'll also need to have at least twice as much memory available (possibly in a different system).

Beware that doing this might be dangerous, depending on how different the Redis versions you are upgrading from and to. At the very least, it should be safe for updates of minor versions of Redis. For major upgrades, each has caveats. Like every other maintenance operation, make sure to test before doing it on your production servers.

4.5. Backing Up Redis

Problem

One issue comes up frequently when talking about NoSQL databases is backing up your data. The notion that these are hard to back up, however, is mostly a misperception since most of the techniques that you'd use to backup a relational database can also be used for NoSQL databases.

If, for some distributed databases, grabbing a point-in-time snapshot of your data might be tricky, this is certainly not the case with Redis. In this section, we'll explain how to achieve it depending on which Redis persistence model you're using. We'll assume you're running your servers on Linux, although filesystem-specific functionality might also be available for other platforms.

Solution

Our proposed solution is heavily dependent on your Redis persistence model:

- With the default persistence model (snapshotting), you're best off using a snapshot as a backup.
- If you're using only AOF, you'll have to back up your log in order to be able to replay it on startup.

It's up to you to store your backup properly. Ideally, you'll store at least a couple of copies of it, have at least one offsite, and do it in a fully automated way. We'll try to explain how to do backups for the different persistance models, but be sure to test your own procedures. Be sure to also test your recovery procedures regularly.

Keep in mind that backing up your data might increase the strain on your production systems. It's probably a good idea to perform the backups on a slave Redis instance, and to actually have slaves running at all times because promoting a new server to master is probably quicker than restoring a backup.

Discussion

Snapshotting

Snapshotting is the default Redis persistance model. As mentioned earlier, depending on your settings, Redis will persist its data to disk if *m* keys changed in *n* seconds. When using this persistence mode, performing a backup is really simple. All you have to do is copy the current snapshot to another location.

 Use a copy, not a move, because if Redis crashes and restarts and the snapshot is not there, you will end up losing all your data! However, keep in mind that you should disable snapshotting while you're copying the file; otherwise, you could end up with a corrupted backup.

In case you want an up-to-date snapshot (instead of using the last one Redis did according to your settings) you can trigger it by issuing:

```
redis-cli BGSAVE
```

and then waiting for the dump file to be updated. Be sure to compress the snapshot before backing it up. That will probably reduce its size by at least a factor of 10.

Restoring a snapshot file is also quite simple. Simply shut down the server, put the snapshot you want to restore in the dbfilename location configured by *redis.conf*, and then start the server. This order is important, because when Redis shuts down, it performs a snapshot, thus overwriting this file.

Append-Only Log (AOF)

If you're using the AOF as the only persistence mode (you can also use it together with snapshotting) the easiest way to do a backup is still to perform use a snapshot as described in the previous section. However, if you're using AOF, you're most likely worried about losing data between snapshots. You may also be avoiding snapshots because they put too much load on your server.

In order to recover when using the AOF, just do the same procedure you would for snapshotting, but instead put your backup in the AOF location. On startup, Redis will simply replay the log.

Be sure to remember to run BGREWRITEAOF regularly if you're using AOF.

Should your Redis server refuse to start due to a corrupted AOF—which can happen if the server crashes or is killed while writing to the file—you can use the `redis-check-aof` utility to fix your AOF:

```
redis-check-aof --fix filename
```

4.6. High Availability with Sentinel

Problem

As with any other distributed system, when you develop applications or services using Redis, you're introducing a new possible point of failure. Given that—until the release of Redis Cluster—you're probably relying on a single master instance, so a failure in that node or server could cause downtime or a service disruption.

Solution

Sentinel was released with Redis 2.6. Redis Sentinel is a distributed monitoring system that continuously checks the state of your Redis instances and performs automatic failover, allowing Sentinel-aware clients to reconnect to the new master. This makes your applications more resilient to failures, because they can recover quickly if you have at least one running slave that can be promoted to master.

Discussion

In order to use Sentinel, you need to use a configuration file:

```
sentinel monitor master-name ip redis-port quorum
        sentinel down-after-milliseconds master-name milliseconds
        sentinel failover-timeout master-name milliseconds
        sentinel parallel-syncs master-name numslaves
```

Start Sentinel with:

```
redis-server /path/to/sentinel.conf --sentinel
```

Sentinel will fetch the running slaves from your master and start monitoring your cluster.

Keep in mind that the `quorum` is the minimum amount of Sentinel nodes that need to agree in order for a Redis master server to be considered down and trigger a failover. You should therefore have at least the same number of Sentinel nodes as specified in your `quorum`, preferably more.

You can also define multiple masters for your Sentinels to watch. For more in-depth information, please refer to the sample Sentinel configuration file (*https://github.com/ antirez/redis/blob/unstable/sentinel.conf*).

In order for your application to be Sentinel-aware and be able to continue operating in a failover scenario, your clients must communicate directly with the Sentinel nodes using the Redis protocol. This is made easier by using a Sentinel-aware client, such as redis-sentinel (*https://github.com/flyerhzm/redis-sentinel*), which will reconnect to the new master in the event of a failover.

You can use `redis-sentinel` in the exact same way you'd use a regular Redis client, except that instead of providing a host and port for your Redis master, you provide a *master-name* and a list of Sentinel nodes:

```
require 'redis-sentinel'

$r = Redis.new(master_name: "master-name",
            sentinels: [{host: "first-sentinel-host", port: 26379},
                        {host: "second-sentinel-host", port: 26380}])
```

4.7. Sharding Redis

Problem

Sharding is a horizontal partitioning tecnique often used with databases. It allows you to scale them by distributing your data across several database instances. Not only does this allow you to have a bigger dataset, as you can use more memory, it will also help if CPU usage is the problem, since you can distribute your instances through different servers (or servers with multiple CPUs).

In Redis's case, sharding can be easily implemented in the client library or application.

Solution

Because Redis Cluster is still under development and should only be released sometime in late 2014, sharding is a useful tecnique for scaling your application when your data no longer fits in a single server.

Currently there are three possibilities when it comes to sharding Redis databases:

Use a client with built-in sharding support
> At this point, most Redis clients don't support sharding. Notable exceptions are:

> > redis-rb (*https://github.com/redis/redis-rb*), a Ruby client
> > Predis (*https://github.com/nrk/predis*), a PHP client
> > Redisent (*https://github.com/jdp/redisent*), a PHP client
> > Rediska (*https://github.com/Shumkov/Rediska*), a PHP client
> > Jedis (*https://github.com/xetorthio/jedis*), a Java client
> > scala-redis (*https://github.com/debasishg/scala-redis*), a Scala client
> > redis-shard (*https://github.com/blindsey/redis-shard*), a Node.js library

Build sharding support yourself on top of an existing client
This involves some programming that might not be too hard if you understand your dataset and applications thoroughly. At the very least, you'll have to implement a partitioning rule and handle the connections to the different servers.

Use a proxy that speaks the Redis protocol and does the sharding for you
Redis Sharding (*https://github.com/kni/redis-sharding*) is a multiplexed proxy that provides sharding to any Redis client. Instead of connecting directly to your Redis servers, you start a proxy and connect to it instead. Unfortunately at this moment, sharding doesn't support resharding on the fly, so you'll be unable to change the configuration of the cluster with the proxy running.

Discussion

If you decide to implement sharding yourself, you should probably use consistent hashing (*http://en.wikipedia.org/wiki/Consistent_hashing*). This will ensure a minimal amount of remapping if you add or remove shards.

Sharding doesn't remove the need for replication. Make sure your cluster is redundant so that the loss of a server doesn't imply any loss of data. Jeremy Zawodny described (*http://bit.ly/at_craigslist/*) on his blog the setup used at Craiglist, and Salvatore has written (*http://antirez.com/post/redis-presharding.html*) on the subject as well.

Something else to keep in mind is that (depending on your implementation) you will not be able to perform some operations that affect multiple keys, because those keys might be in different shards (servers). If you rely on these operations, you'll need to adjust your hashing algorithm to ensure that all the required keys will always be in the same shard.

Finding Help

Should you find yourself in need of help with Redis or having problems, questions, or doubts, there are several ways of reaching out for help and the Redis community is very friendly and helpful.

- *http://redis.io*

  This is the Redis official site. There you'll be able to find the latest documentation, command reference, articles, tutorials, downloads, and everything Redis-related.

  The site (*https://github.com/antirez/redis-io*) itself and the documentation (*https://github.com/antirez/redis-doc*) it contains are GitHub projects. Should you find any omissions or bugs, please contribute to this community effort.

- Mailing List

  The Redis Mailing List (*http://groups.google.com/group/redis-db*) is very active, and with more than 1500 members you're bound to find someone that can help you. If you have questions that the documentation can't answer or need some tips on how to solve a specific problem, try searching or emailing the list.

  Given the volume of email messages that the list gets everyday, it's without doubt one of the best places to find information on Redis. Start by searching the existing topics (*http://groups.google.com/group/redis-db/topics*).

- IRC Channel

  If you prefer to use IRC, you can also try the #redis IRC channel on Freenode (*http://webchat.freenode.net/?channels=redis*).

- StackOverflow

  StackOverflow (*http://stackoverflow.com/*) is a Q&A site oriented towards programming issues. While the Redis mailing list is probably the best option for Redis related questions, if you're a StackOverflow user you can use the "redis" tag (*http://bit.ly/redis_tag*) when posting.

About the Authors

Tiago Macedo is a Berlin-based developer that has been working with Redis for a few years. He has worked at several startups, like Wimdu, 3scale Networks, Soocial and Webreakstuff.

Fred Oliveira is a developer and designer hybrid. After living in Silicon Valley to work with Techcrunch and Edgeio, Fred started Webreakstuff (a design, development, and strategy consultancy) to provide services to companies and individuals. He is the co-founder of the Web 2.0 Workgroup with Michael Arrington and Richard MacManus and a 2005 Google Summer of Code alumnus. These days his main focus is to craft online experiences and help his clients build successful web-based products and services. He is also an advisor to several startups and a mentor at 500 Startups, a seed fund and startup accelerator out of Mountain View, California.

Colophon

The animal on the cover of *Redis Cookbook* is a mouse opossum.

The cover image is from *Johnson's Natural History*. The cover font is Adobe ITC Garamond. The text font is Linotype Birka; the heading font is Adobe Myriad Condensed; and the code font is LucasFont's TheSansMonoCondensed.

Have it your way.

Get even more for your money.

Join the O'Reilly Community, and register the O'Reilly books you own. It's free, and you'll get:

- $4.99 ebook upgrade offer
- 40% upgrade offer on O'Reilly print books
- Membership discounts on books and events
- Free lifetime updates to ebooks and videos
- Multiple ebook formats, DRM FREE
- Participation in the O'Reilly community
- Newsletters
- Account management
- 100% Satisfaction Guarantee

Signing up is easy:

1. Go to: oreilly.com/go/register
2. Create an O'Reilly login.
3. Provide your address.
4. Register your books.

Note: English-language books only

To order books online:
oreilly.com/store

For questions about products or an order:
orders@oreilly.com

To sign up to get topic-specific email announcements and/or news about upcoming books, conferences, special offers, and new technologies:
elists@oreilly.com

For technical questions about book content:
booktech@oreilly.com

To submit new book proposals to our editors:
proposals@oreilly.com

O'Reilly books are available in multiple DRM-free ebook formats. For more information:
oreilly.com/ebooks

CPSIA information can be obtained at www.ICGtesting.com
Printed in the USA
BVOW09s1900210715

409696BV00016B/332/P